Peterson Field Guides®
For Young Naturalists

Shorebirds

Jonathan P. Latimer
Karen Stray Nolting

Illustrations by Roger Tory Peterson

Foreword by Virginia Marie Peterson

Houghton Mifflin Company
Boston 1999

FOREWORD

My husband, Roger Tory Peterson, traced his interest in nature back to an encounter he had with an exhausted flicker when he was only 11 years old. When he found what he thought was a dead bird in a bundle of brown feathers, he touched it and the bird suddenly exploded into life, showing its golden feathers. Roger said it was "like resurrection." That experience was "the crucial moment" that started Roger on a lifelong journey with nature. He combined his passion for nature with his talent as an artist to create a series of field guides and paintings that changed the way people experience the natural world. Roger often spoke of an even larger goal, however. He believed that an understanding of the natural world would lead people — especially young people — to a recognition of "the interconnnectedness of things all over the world." The Peterson Field Guides for Young Naturalists are a continuation of Roger's interest in educating and inspiring young people to see that "life itself is important — not just ourselves, but all life."
—Virginia Marie Peterson

Copyright © 1999 by Houghton Mifflin Company
Foreword copyright © 1999 by Virginia Marie Peterson
All illustrations from *A Field Guide to the Birds* © 1980 by Roger Tory Peterson and
A Field Guide to Western Birds © 1990 by Roger Tory Peterson.

Special thanks to Dick Walton for his expert advice.

Library of Congress Cataloging-in-Publication Data
Latimer, Jonathan P.
Shorebirds / Jonathan P. Latimer & Karen Stray Nolting ; illustrations by Roger Tory Peterson ; foreword, Virginia Marie Peterson. p. cm. — (Peterson field guides for young naturalists)
Summary: A field guide to shorebirds in the air, on the water, on the ground, and in the grass, including gulls, coots, sandpipers, and egrets.
ISBN 0-395-95212-3 (cl). — ISBN 0-395-92278-X (pbk.)
1. Shore birds—Juvenile literature. 2. Shore birds—Identification—Juvenile literature. [1. Shore birds.]
I. Nolting, Karen Stray. II. Peterson, Roger Tory, 1908–1996, ill. III. Title. IV. Series.
QL676.2.L374 1999   598.3'3—dc21   98-35510 CIP AC

Photo Credits
Herring Gull: O. S. Pettingill; Ring-billed Gull: O. S. Pettingill; Caspian Tern: O. S. Pettingill; Brown Pelican: Robert E. Barber; American Coot: Mike Hopiak; Mallard: Lang Elliott; Northern Pintail: Lawrence Wales; Double-crested Cormorant: Christopher Crowley; Canada Goose: D. Robert Franz; Mute Swan: John Gavin; Sanderling: W. A. Paff; Least Sandpiper: Lawrence Wales; Spotted Sandpiper: Mike Hopiak; Killdeer: Mike Hopiak; Common Snipe: Bill Dyer; Greater Yellowlegs: Lawrence Wales; Great Blue Heron: Blaine Ulmer; Black-crowned Night-Heron: Johann Schumacher; Snowy Egret: Jack Murry; Cattle Egret: Lawrence Wales.

Book design by Lisa Diercks. Typeset in Mrs Eaves and Base 9 from Emigre
Manufactured in the United States of America
WOZ 10 9 8 7 6 5 4 3 2 1

CONTENTS

Foreword
Virginia Marie Peterson

How to Watch Birds Along The Shore 4

In the Air
Herring Gull *8*
Ring-billed Gull *10*
Caspian Tern *12*
Brown Pelican *14*

On the Water
Coot *16*
Mallard *18*
Pintail *20*
Double-crested Cormorant *22*
Canada Goose *24*
Swans *26*

On the Ground
Sanderling *28*
Least Sandpiper *30*
Spotted Sandpiper *32*
Killdeer *34*
Common Snipe *36*
Greater Yellowlegs *38*

In the Grass
Great Blue Heron *40*
Black-crowned Night-Heron *42*
Snowy Egret *44*
Cattle Egret *46*

Index & Life List 48

HOW TO WATCH BIRDS ALONG THE SHORE

Birds can be found almost anywhere land and water come together. There are birds along the seacoasts of North America and on the shores of its lakes and ponds. Many birds also live near the banks of rivers and streams or in marshes, swamps, and bogs.

Birds inhabit these places for many reasons. These areas contain thousands of different plants and insects that birds eat. They are also home to shellfish, mollusks, fish, reptiles, and small animals that many birds prey upon. And they provide an abundance of the grasses and other plants that birds use to build their nests.

This book will show you how to recognize some of the birds you are likely to see near the bodies of fresh water and salt water in North America. It uses illustrations by the man who revolutionized bird identification, Roger Tory Peterson. He invented a simple system of drawings and pointers (now known as the "Peterson System") that call attention to the unique marks on each kind of bird. This book introduces the Peterson System to beginners and young birders. It can help you answer the most important question of all: *What kind of bird is that?*

What Kind of Bird Is That?

Figuring out what kind of bird you've seen is like solving a mystery. You gather clues and eventually you can find the answer. Sometimes you need only one or two clues. Other times you need more. Solving the mystery is a challenge, but it is also a lot of fun. Try not to get frustrated. You'll get better with practice. Here are some questions you can ask when trying to identify an unknown bird.

Where Did You See the Bird? Although all the birds in this book can be found near shores, some of them spend much of their time on a beach or in grass, while others float on the water. The birds in this book are organized into the four locations where you are most likely to see them. Gulls are usually seen in the air above the ocean. Ducks are commonly found swimming on freshwater lakes or ponds. But birds can fly anywhere. Don't be surprised if you see gulls far inland or ducks a long way from water.

Migration

In spring many shorebirds migrate north to their nesting sites. In fall they move south to warmer areas where there is more food. Even tiny sandpipers migrate hundreds of miles. This means it is possible to see unusual birds as they pass through your area during these seasons.

How Big Is the Bird?
Size is a quick clue to identifying a bird. Is it larger than a sandpiper? Is it smaller than a swan? The size of the bird will help you exclude some choices and focus on others.

What Is Its Shape? Shape is another clue to identifying a shorebird. Does it have a sharply pointed tail? Then it may be a pintail. Does it have long legs and a very sharp bill? Then it may be a Great Blue Heron.

What Color Is the Bird? Color may be one of the first things you notice when you see a bird. For example, a male Mallard has a green head. But color alone is not always enough to help you identify a shorebird. Many shorebirds are brown or black or white. This can make them difficult to tell apart.

Does It Have Any Field Marks? Shorebirds have marks such as spots or stripes on their feathers, or colored bills or legs. These are called field marks. Field marks can be found on a bird's head, wings, body, or tail. A Killdeer, for instance, has two black bands across its chest.

As you get used to looking at birds, noticing field marks will become a very quick way to identify them or to tell similar birds apart. Both Snowy Egrets and Cattle Egrets are white, but only Snowy Egrets have bright yellow feet.

What Is the Bird Doing? As you watch birds you may notice that they behave in certain ways. Some of these behaviors are good clues to the bird's identity. If you see a white bird hovering over the ocean, it is probably a tern or a gull. If you see a small bird running in and out with the waves on a beach like a little wind-up toy, it is probably a Sanderling. As you become more familiar with birds, you will be able to identify them by their behavior alone.

What Does It Sound Like? Some birds have calls or songs that can be recognized immediately. The quack of a duck or the honk of a goose are familiar sounds. Some birds even say their own names. Listen for the *kill-deeah* of a Killdeer.

HERRING GULL

The sight of gulls wheeling overhead and the sound of their noisy screams — these are two of the most familiar signs of the seashore. Herring Gulls are large white gulls with yellow bills and gray wings tipped with black.

Herring Gulls search for their food by walking around, swimming, or flying. Sometimes they settle on the water and dip their heads in to pick up something. Often gulls with food in their bill will be chased by other gulls that are trying to steal it.

You may see adult Herring Gulls in the company of brown gulls. These are usually young Herring Gulls. It takes three to four years before a young Herring Gull takes on the white and gray look of an adult.

Did You Know?
- Herring Gulls carry clams and other shellfish high in the air and drop them to break open their shells.
- At sea Herring Gulls often follow fishing boats or feed on fish driven to the surface by tuna or whales.
- Herring Gulls can drink either salt water or fresh water.

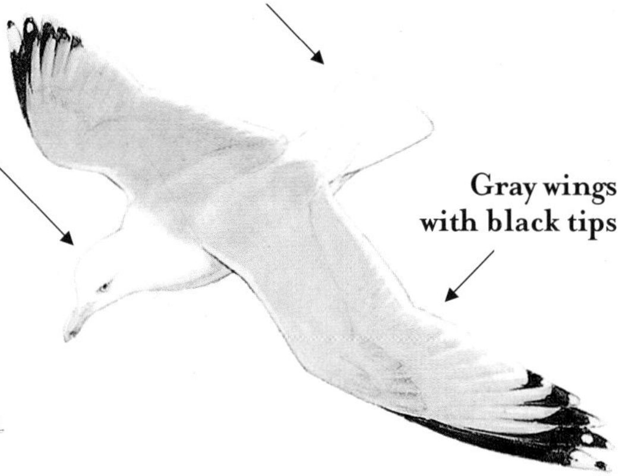

White tail

White head

Gray wings
with black tips

Yellow bill with
a red spot

White spots called
"mirrors" on wingtips

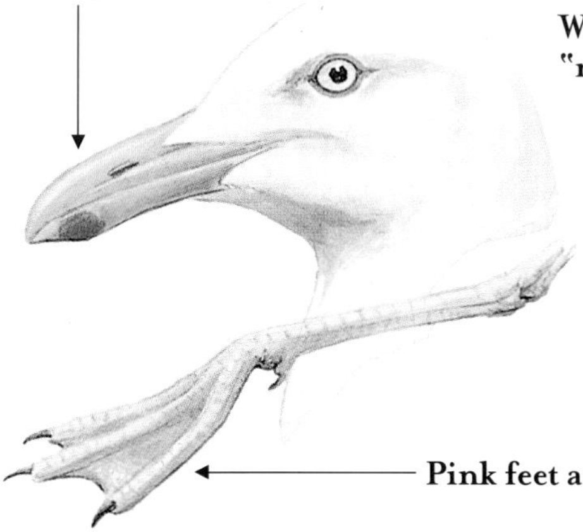

Males and females
look alike.

Pink feet and legs

Habitat Herring Gulls are found along the ocean
coast, around bays, beaches, and harbors. They can also
be seen in farmland and around dumps.

Voice The loud call of the Herring Gull sounds like
hiyak . . . hiyah . . . hyiah-hyak or *yuk-yuk-yuk-yuk-yuckle-yuckle.*
When they are distressed, their call sounds like *gah-gah-gah.*

Food Herring Gulls will eat almost anything. They
often scavenge garbage, but they also eat fish, shellfish,
sea urchins, and other birds and eggs.

RING-BILLED GULL

Although the Ring-billed Gull is considered a shore-bird, it is the gull you are most likely to spot far from the shore. Flocks of Ring-billed Gulls are often found inland around freshwater lakes, city parking lots, and farmers' fields. They also gather on the grass around airport runways. Unfortunately, this has led to a number of collisions between Ring-billed Gulls and airplanes.

Ring-billed Gulls are more likely than Herring Gulls to gather in large flocks, even when they are not nesting. These flocks can contain thousands of birds.

Ring-billed Gulls search for food in lots of ways — by flying, walking around, wading, and swimming. They also often gather at garbage dumps to hunt for scraps.

Did You Know?
- The gulls you see outside fast-food restaurants are almost always Ring-billed Gulls.
- Like other gulls, it takes young Ring-billed Gulls three years to develop adult plumage. Young Ring-billed Gulls are brown and usually have a narrow dark band near the end of their pale tail.
- A colony of nesting Ring-billed Gulls on an island in Ontario was estimated to number 85,000 pairs.

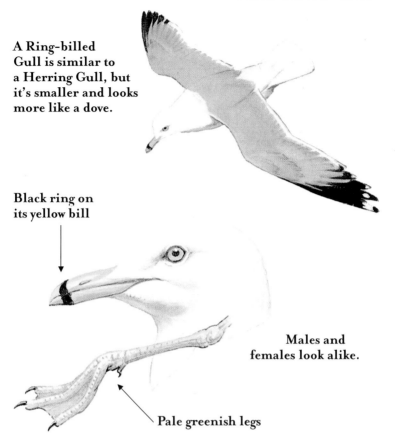

A Ring-billed Gull is similar to a Herring Gull, but it's smaller and looks more like a dove.

Black ring on its yellow bill

Males and females look alike.

Pale greenish legs

Habitat Ring-billed Gulls are found along the ocean coasts, on docks, and around bays. They are also seen near lakes, dumps, plowed fields, and cities.

Voice The loud call of a Ring-billed Gull is similar to a Herring Gull but higher. It sounds like a shrill *hiyak*.

Food Ring-billed Gulls will eat almost anything, including insects, rodents, earthworms, grain, and garbage. They also eat food scraps fed to them by people.

CASPIAN TERN

There are several kinds of terns in North America — and they are easy to spot. These graceful water birds look more streamlined than gulls or other shorebirds. They have sharp-pointed wings and forked tails like swallows.

Terns swoop over the water with their bill pointing downward. When they see their prey, they hover above the water, flapping their wings very fast. Suddenly they plunge into the water and out again, often with a fish in their bill.

The Caspian Tern is the largest tern in North America, but it is still only about the size of a medium gull. Unlike other terns, Caspian Terns usually fish alone. They are known as the least sociable of the terns.

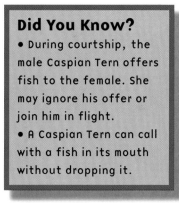

Did You Know?
- During courtship, the male Caspian Tern offers fish to the female. She may ignore his offer or join him in flight.
- A Caspian Tern can call with a fish in its mouth without dropping it.

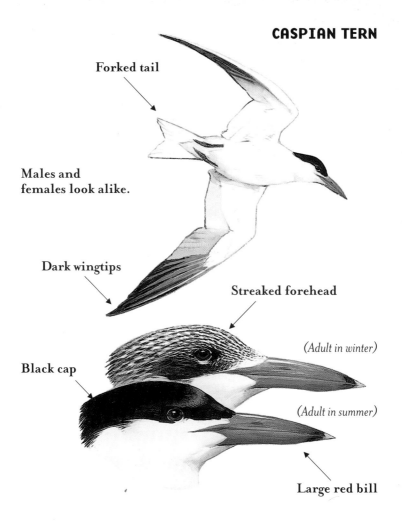

Forked tail

Males and
females look alike.

Dark wingtips

Streaked forehead

(Adult in winter)

Black cap

(Adult in summer)

Large red bill

Habitat Caspian Terns nest throughout the world.
They live near large lakes and ocean shores. They hunt
in fresh water and salt water and are most often found in
protected bays or lagoons.

Voice The hoarse, low call of the Caspian Tern sounds
like *kraa-uh* or *karr*. They also make repeated *kaks* as they fly.

Food Terns eat all kinds of small fish, including mullet, alewives, and shiner perch.

BROWN PELICAN

A pelican's pouch can hold up to three times more than its stomach can! When it catches its prey, it opens its bill and grabs a mouthful of fish and as much as 3 gallons of water. The pelican holds the fish in its pouch while the water drains out. Then the pelican tosses its head back and swallows the fish.

Brown Pelicans hunt by gliding over the ocean with slow, powerful wingbeats. They have very good eyesight, and when they spot a fish they plunge bill-first into the water. They often dive again and again in the same place. Gulls sometimes chase Brown Pelicans, trying to steal the fish they have caught.

Did You Know?
• Brown Pelicans are not only excellent divers, they are also good swimmers. They have been timed swimming at 3 miles per hour.
• Brown Pelicans gather in large flocks during much of the year. They nest in large colonies on the ground, in bushes, or in the tops of trees.
• Although an adult Brown Pelican can weigh as much as 10 pounds and have a wingspan of over 6 feet, it is the smallest member of the pelican family.

BROWN PELICAN

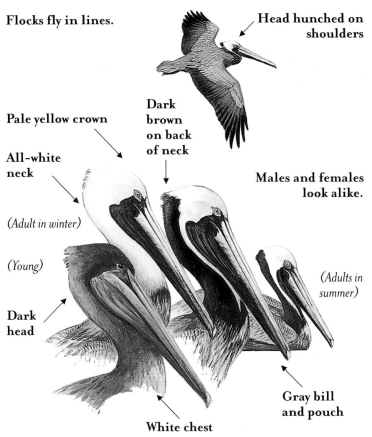

Flocks fly in lines.

Head hunched on shoulders

Pale yellow crown

Dark brown on back of neck

All-white neck

(Adult in winter)

(Young)

Males and females look alike.

(Adults in summer)

Dark head

Gray bill and pouch

White chest

Habitat Brown Pelicans are found along the coasts of the Atlantic and Pacific Oceans and the Gulf of Mexico, especially near shallow bays.

Voice Adult Brown Pelicans are usually silent, although they sometimes give a low croak. Young pelicans in the nest make a squealing sound.

Food Brown Pelicans are primarily fish eaters and require up to 4 pounds of fish a day. Most of the fish that pelicans eat are not considered commercially important. They include mullet, minnows, and silversides.

COOT

Have you ever heard the old-fashioned saying "crazier than a coot"? No one knows for sure where it came from, but it could come from the wacky way coots take off from water. They begin by running as hard as they can. Their large toes help lift them out of the water. At the same time, they beat their wings furiously. They splash faster and faster and eventually become airborne. This takeoff lasts only a moment, but it looks very crazy.

Although they resemble ducks, coots are not nearly as graceful. They are sometimes called "splatterers" because of their wet and wild takeoffs. When swimming, they pump their heads back and forth. They also bob up and down when they walk.

Coots skitter across the water
when they take off.

Paler than adults

Duller colored bill

Dark gray body

Black
head

(Young)

White
bill

(Adult)

White patch
under tail

(Coot chick)

Habitat Most of the year coots are found near ponds,
lakes, and marshes. In winter they can also be seen on
saltwater bays, on fields, and even on golf courses.

Voice Coots make a
number of cackling or
croaking sounds. Their
call is a grating *kuk–kuk–
kuk–kuk* or *kakakakakaka.*

Food Coots eat mostly
algae, plants, and grasses
that they find in the water.
They also eat insects, tadpoles, and small fish.

Did You Know?
• Coots can use their
feet to grasp things.
• Coots sometimes steal
food from ducks and
even from swans, which
are much larger than
coots.
• The coot's official
name is American Coot.

MALLARD

There are more Mallards than any other wild duck in North America. They are found on most freshwater ponds and lakes. The green head of the male Mallard makes him one of the easiest birds to identify.

Mallards feed off the bottom in shallow water. They tip their heads down and pick seeds out of the mud. On land they eat grass or seed and also dig for roots. In parks some Mallards thrive on handouts from people.

Mallards migrate throughout fall and return in early spring. They form pairs in winter, and females probably lead males to the nesting area. Within a day after the ducklings are hatched, the mother takes them to water. There the young are protected by the female, but they feed themselves.

Did You Know?
- When Mallards are alarmed, they jump straight out of the water and take flight.
- It is estimated that there are more than 9 million Mallards in North America.
- Mallards are the ancestors of most types of domesticated ducks.

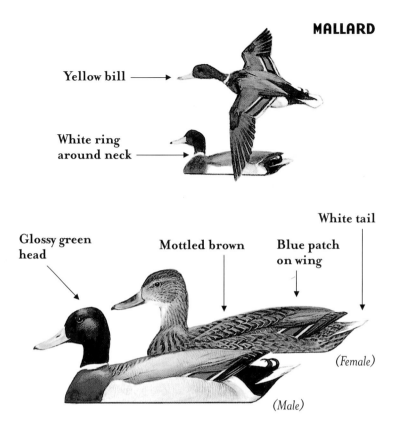

Yellow bill ——→

White ring around neck ——→

Glossy green head

Mottled brown

Blue patch on wing

White tail

(Female)

(Male)

Habitat Mallards can be seen on almost any body of fresh water. They live in marshes and swamps and on ponds, lakes, and rivers. They are also found in parks and grain fields.

Voice Female Mallards quack loudly. Males make calls that sounds like *yeeb* or a low *kwek.*

Food Mallards eat a wide variety of food, including the seeds and roots of all kinds of marsh plants. They also eat insects, snails, tadpoles, frogs, earthworms, and small fish. They often eat grain or rice left after harvest in farmers' fields.

PINTAIL

Pintails are so afraid of people that they are usually seen only at a distance. Fortunately, their long needle-pointed tail feathers and long necks are easy to identify. This is especially true when they dip their heads underwater to feed and point their tails up in the air.

When taking off from water, pintails leap into the air. When landing, they spread their wings to slow down. This allows them to feed on very small ponds that have little room for taking off or landing.

Fast and graceful fliers, pintails travel over a wide area to find food. They also migrate in flocks over long distances. Some pintails have even flown from Utah to Hawaii. Others fly from Siberia to winter in North America.

Did You Know?
- Pintails have been timed flying at over 50 miles per hour.
- If a pintail's nest is approached by an intruder, the female will pretend to be injured to draw the intruder away.
- The pintail's official name is Northern Pintail.

The pintail is a slender
duck with a slim neck.

The pintail is the only duck
found on fresh water that has
a long pointed tail.

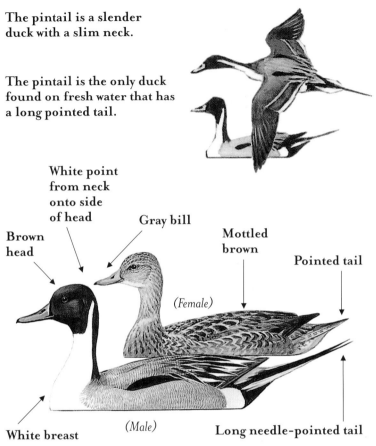

White point
from neck
onto side
of head

Gray bill

Brown
head

Mottled
brown

Pointed tail

(Female)

White breast

(Male)

Long needle-pointed tail

Habitat Pintails can be found inland on ponds,
marshes, and prairies. They also can be seen on saltwater
bays along the coasts of North America.

Voice Female pintails call with a low *quack*. Males call
with a whistling *prrip, prrip.*

Food Like Mallards, pintails dabble in shallow water
for seeds and grasses. They also eat insects, snails and
other mollusks, crabs, crayfish, and minnows.

DOUBLE-CRESTED CORMORANT

When they are not in the water, cormorants stand on rocks or posts, often with their wings held open. Because their feathers are not completely waterproof, they hold their wings open to dry them when they first come out of the water. When swimming, these diving

birds float very low in the water, with just their head and neck sticking up above the surface.

Cormorants are excellent at fishing. They hunt by sight and can see well in the air and underwater. They fly just above the surface of the water. When they spot a fish, they dive in and chase it underwater, paddling quickly with their webbed feet.

Did You Know?

- The cormorant seen most often is the Double-crested Cormorant. Its name refers to the two small tufts of feathers on its head that appear only for a short time during nesting season.
- Cormorants usually stay underwater for 30 seconds to a minute each time they dive. During that time they have been known to go as deep as 70 to 100 feet.
- The Double-crested Cormorant is the only cormorant you are likely to see near inland lakes and rivers.

DOUBLE-CRESTED CORMORANT

Young paler underneath

Cormorants are often seen sitting straight up on rocks or posts near water.

Slender yellow bill hooked at end

Yellow chin

Sometimes spreads wings to dry them

Males and females look alike.

Pale chest with dark belly

Dark webbed feet

Habitat Cormorants can be seen along the ocean from rocky northern coasts to southern sandy beaches and mangrove swamps.

Voice Although they are usually silent, cormorants sometimes make low grunts when they are in their nesting colony.

Food Cormorants hunt fish, but they also eat crabs, shrimp, crayfish, frogs, and eels. Sometimes they eat mollusks, snakes, and plants found in the water.

CANADA GOOSE

For many people, the honking of Canada Geese flying overhead in V-formation is one of the signs of the changing seasons. It was once thought that these formations were led by a "wise old" male, but it is now known that females often lead. Though the lead changes as the flock flies, males tend to follow.

Canada Geese take off from water by running a few steps and then lifting themselves with slow, powerful strokes of their wings. When they land on water, they stick their feet out beneath them and use them like skis.

Canada Geese develop strong family ties. They may mate for life, returning to the same nesting site each year.

Did You Know?
- A Canada Goose can weigh up to 24 pounds.
- In some areas, the number of Canada Geese has increased so much that they are now considered a nuisance.

Canada Geese
often fly in
V-formation.

Long black neck

White
patch
on chin

Males and females
look alike.

Pale breast

Habitat Canada Geese can be found on lakes, ponds, bays, and marshes, or in fields nearby. They can also be seen in parks and on lawns in cities and suburbs.

Voice The call of the Canada Goose is a loud honking or barking that sounds like *ka-ronk* or *ka-lunk*. They may also hiss threateningly when approached.

Food Canada Geese graze on plants that they find in the water or on the ground. They sometimes eat insects, mollusks, and worms.

SWANS

These beautiful birds often appear in fairy tales and stories. Swans are the largest water birds, and their long necks make them easy to identify. Although wild swans are not found in many parts of North America, you may see a Mute Swan or a Tundra Swan.

The Mute Swan is the one most often seen in parks. In the 1800s, Mute Swans were brought from Europe as decorations for large estates in New York. Many escaped and now live in the wild. You can easily recognize their bright orange bills.

Tundra Swans are smaller than Mute Swans and have black bills. Tundra Swans are native to North America. They migrate from their nesting sites near the Arctic Circle and spend summer in several places in the United States and Canada.

Did You Know?
- Swans mate for life and both parents care for their young. Young swans sometimes ride on a parent's back.
- The Mute Swan is the royal swan of England.
- Tundra Swans are also known as Whistling Swans because of their call.

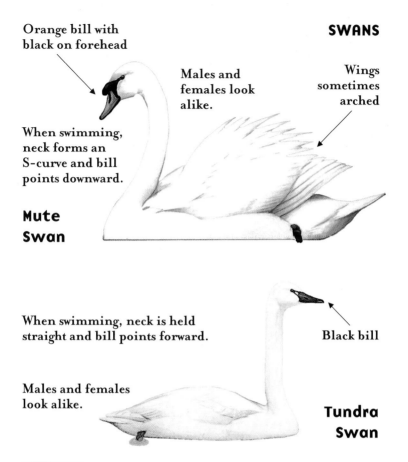

SWANS

Orange bill with black on forehead

Males and females look alike.

Wings sometimes arched

When swimming, neck forms an S-curve and bill points downward.

Mute Swan

When swimming, neck is held straight and bill points forward.

Black bill

Males and females look alike.

Tundra Swan

Habitat Swans can be found on both fresh water and salt water. You may see them on ponds, lakes, and large rivers or in bays or coastal lagoons.

Voice The Mute Swan is not really mute. Its call is a soft but harsh bark, and it hisses when threatened. You are more likely to hear the humming sound of its wings beating, which can be heard as far as half a mile away. The Tundra Swan makes a high cooing call and its wings are silent.

Food Swans eat plants found in water. They sometimes eat grain from harvested fields.

SANDERLING

Sanderlings are lots of fun to watch on a sandy beach. They race in and out with the waves like little wind-up toys. As a wave goes out, they run behind it, pecking at the wet sand, searching for food. When another wave rolls in, they quickly retreat, running just in front of the oncoming water.

Sanderlings are among the champions at migration. They nest in the Far North during summer, near the Arctic Circle. In fall some Sanderlings migrate south along the Atlantic Coast then cross to the Pacific Coast and spend winter on beaches in Chile and Peru. They return north in spring, flying along the Pacific Coast to their Arctic nesting ground. Many Sanderlings return to the same nesting ground year after year.

Did You Know?
- Flocks of Sanderlings spread out in a line along the water's edge. Small groups follow each wave in and out.
- Sanderlings may be seriously endangered. Some studies suggest that their numbers have dropped by more than 80 percent since the 1970s because of land development along their migration routes.

SANDERLING

Gray back

White underneath

White stripe on wings

Rusty brown back

Rusty brown head

Plump body

Black bill

(Summer)

Males and females look alike.

(Winter)

The whitest sandpiper

Black legs

Habitat Sanderlings are found on most sandy ocean beaches all over the world. They are sometimes seen on rocky shores or mudflats and on beaches of inland lakes, especially during winter.

Voice The call of a Sanderling is usually made when it is flying. It sounds like a sharp *twick* or *quit*. Sanderlings also chatter when feeding.

Food Sanderlings hunt for tiny crabs, mollusks, insects, and worms in the sand.

LEAST SANDPIPER

L ook closely at the flocks of small birds walking on the mudflats in many marshy areas. These little birds are most likely sandpipers. They are sometimes called "peep" sandpipers because of the sounds they make. Sandpipers are difficult to tell apart, even up close. But if you see one that is about the size of a sparrow and you notice that it has yellowish or greenish — not black — legs, it will be a Least Sandpiper.

Least Sandpipers walk slowly along the ground looking for small insects or tiny crustaceans to eat. They frequently pause and pick up their prey or probe the soft mud or sand with their bills. When they are frightened, they fly off in a zigzag pattern.

Did You Know?
• If you stand quietly, a Least Sandpiper may come very close as it searches for food.
• Flocks of Least Sandpipers fly in very tight formations, moving together in amazing unison. A flock may seem to change color as the Least Sandpipers twist and turn, revealing their dark backs or pale bellies.

Males and females look alike.

A Least Sandpiper is about the size of a sparrow.

Smaller and darker brown than other shorebirds

Thin bill

(Winter)

(Summer)

Yellowish or greenish legs and feet

Streaked breast

Habitat Least Sandpipers are often seen near small bodies of water — even by the pools of water left after it rains. They can be found on mudflats and in grassy marshes. Near the ocean, Least Sandpipers are usually found on tidal marshes rather than on sandy beaches.

Voice One way to tell a Least Sandpiper from other peeps is by the sound it makes. Its call is a thin *kree-eet.*

Food Least Sandpipers hunt tiny animals that live in mud or sand. These include sand fleas, insect larvae, small snails, and worms.

SPOTTED SANDPIPER

These sandpipers are just a little larger than sparrows, but they are easy to recognize. When Spotted Sandpipers walk, they teeter along, bobbing their tail up and down as though they were having trouble keeping their balance. They are also the sandpiper you are most likely to see near small lakes and streams.

Spotted Sandpipers are usually seen in pairs or in small groups. They climb over rocks and logs looking for food. When startled, they fly low over the water, calling clearly. They beat their wings rapidly, then glide for a short distance with their wings held stiffly in a bowed shape. Spotted Sandpipers can swim, but they usually stay out of the water.

Did You Know?

• The female Spotted Sandpiper is larger and more aggressive than the male.

• Not only can Spotted Sandpipers swim, they have also been known to dive underwater to escape hawks.

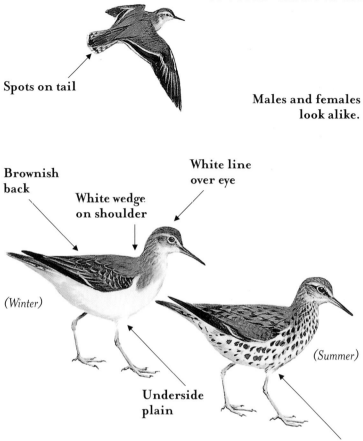

Spots on tail

Males and females
look alike.

Brownish
back

White wedge
on shoulder

White line
over eye

(Winter)

Underside
plain

(Summer)

Large round brown or
black spots on chest

Habitat Spotted Sandpipers can be seen on the shores of lakes and ponds and along rivers and streams. They are also found at the seashore and in open fields.

Voice The call of the Spotted Sandpiper is a clear *peet* or *peet-weet!* or sometimes *pee-weet-weet-weet-weet.*

Food Spotted Sandpipers hunt a variety of insects along the shore and even catch some in the air. They also eat crabs, crayfish, small fish, and earthworms.

KILLDEER

Killdeers are noisy birds that spend most of their time on the ground. They often run a few steps, then stop and peck at insects. Then they run a few more steps and stop again.

Killdeers have developed a special way of protecting their young. If an intruder comes too close, a parent will pretend to be injured to lure the intruder away. The adult Killdeer will drag itself along the ground, often with one wing open as though it were broken. The Killdeer will stay just out of reach until it feels its young are safe. Then it will suddenly recover and fly away.

These shorebirds are also found far from the shore.

Did You Know?
- Unlike other shorebirds, Killdeers do not probe in the mud with their bills to find food. They find it by sight.
- The Killdeer's nest is usually a shallow furrow dug on open ground. They sometimes nest on gravel roofs of buildings.
- Killdeer have been timed flying at 55 miles per hour and running at 5 miles per hour.

Males and females look alike.

Golden patch on rear

Short straight bill similar to a pigeon's

Round head

(Adult)

Two black bands across chest

(Chick)

One band across chest

Habitat Although a shorebird, Killdeers can also be found on farmland and in the country, along river banks, and even around airports.

Voice Killdeers get their name from their noisy call, a repeated *kill-deeah*. They also make several other sounds, including a sad *dee-ee* or *dee-dee-dee*.

Food Almost the only thing Killdeers eat is insects, including grasshoppers, caterpillars, ants, and flies.

COMMON SNIPE

Common Snipes spend a lot of their time alone searching for food in marshes or bogs. They are most active in the early morning and the late afternoon. Although the tip of their bill is hard, the bill itself is flexible and very sensitive to touch. When a Common Snipe hunts, it plunges its bill into soft earth or mud. When it detects prey, the snipe can quickly snap it up.

During nesting season male Common Snipes fly in circles at a height of more than 300 feet, then make shallow dives at high speed. During the dive, their tail feathers produce a deep booming noise that sounds like *huhuhuhuhuhuhu*. This noise can be heard up to half a mile away.

Did You Know?
- After the young Common Snipes have hatched, their parents may split the brood between them, each taking care of half the chicks.
- Common Snipes migrate in flocks at night.

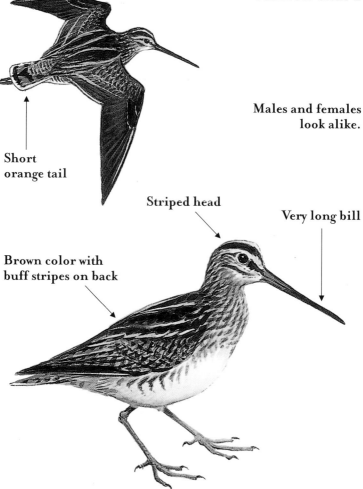

Males and females
look alike.

Short
orange tail

Striped head

Very long bill

Brown color with
buff stripes on back

Habitat Common Snipes are found throughout the world in damp areas such as freshwater and saltwater marshes, bogs, and wet meadows.

Voice The raspy call of the Common Snipe sounds like *scaip*. Its song sound like *chip-a, chip-a, chip-a.*

Food Common Snipes hunt insects and earthworms that burrow in damp soil or live in shallow water.

GREATER YELLOWLEGS

If you come too close to a group of sandpipers, the first one to sound the alarm and fly away is likely to be a Greater Yellowlegs. Its loud call will probably frighten off other shore-birds nearby. If you can get close enough, you may see a Greater Yellowlegs bob its body up and down as it walks.

The Greater Yellowlegs usually hunts for food in small pools or on mudflats, but it does not probe in the mud like other sandpipers. Instead, Greater Yellowlegs wade or swim in shallow water. They swing the tip of their long bill from side to side in the water to skim off food, or they pick their food off the surface.

GREATER YELLOWLEGS

Dark wings

White tail

Long slightly upturned bill

Back checkered with gray, black, and white

Males and females look alike.

If you see a bird that looks like a Greater Yellowlegs but is smaller, it may be a Lesser Yellowlegs.

Bright yellow legs

Habitat Greater Yellowlegs can be found on ocean mudflats, on freshwater and saltwater marshes, and near ponds and lakes.

Voice The call of the Greater Yellowlegs is a whistle with three notes that sounds like *whew-whew-whew* or *dear! dear! dear!*

Food Greater Yellowlegs eat mostly insects and small fish. They also eat snails, tadpoles, and sometimes berries.

GREAT BLUE HERON

The Great Blue Heron is a patient hunter. It will stand very still in shallow water, waiting for its prey to come close. When a fish or a frog passes by, this huge blue bird will stab at it with its long sharp bill. If the heron spears it, it will lift its prey out of the water and, with a toss of its head, devour it.

After a while, the Great Blue Heron will shift its position, stepping carefully with its long skinny legs to avoid scaring its prey. If it is disturbed, the heron will take off slowly and fly to another spot. When it flies, it folds its neck into an S-curve, hunching its head on its shoulders. Its long legs trail behind.

Did You Know?

• The Great Blue Heron is the largest heron in North America. Adults can be 4 feet tall and have a wingspread of 7 feet.

• As they grow older, Great Blue Herons get better at hunting.

• Great Blue Herons sometimes dive into deep water to catch fish.

Herons fly with their necks pulled in. A crane flies with its neck straight out, like a goose.

Black cap

(Young)

Black eye streak and plume

Long yellow bill

Bluish body with lighter neck and head

(Adult)

A very large bird, it stands 4 feet tall.

Males and females look alike, but males are slightly larger.

Habitat Great Blue Herons are found near almost any calm fresh water, including marshes, swamps, and slow-moving rivers. They are also seen in shallow coastal bays and tidal flats.

Voice The loud croaking call of a Great Blue Herons sounds like *frahnk, frahnk, frahnk.*

Food Great Blue Herons eat mostly fish, but they also hunt a wide variety other animals, including frogs, turtles, snakes, rodents, birds, and insects.

BLACK-CROWNED NIGHT-HERON

About the time other herons and egrets are returning from a day of hunting to roost for the night, Black-crowned Night-Herons are just starting out. They hunt for their prey at night, which is how they got their name. During the day night-herons roost in flocks, usually in trees or tall bushes near the water's edge.

In nesting season, flocks of Black-crowned Night-Herons can be very large. At first it may look like there are many more adults than young. This is because the colors of the feathers of the young night-herons blend into the background vegetation so well. If the flock is startled and takes flight, you will see that there are usually many more young than adults.

Did You Know?
• Black-crowned Night-Herons sometimes greet each other by stretching their necks and touching their bills.
• Black-crowned Night-Herons roost by themselves and are rarely found in mixed flocks with other herons or egrets.
• Unlike other herons, young night-herons look very different from their parents.

BLACK-CROWNED NIGHT-HERON

Black cap

Black back

White chest

Males and females look alike.

(Adult)

Gray wings and tail

Brown with white and buff spots and streaks

(Young)

Habitat Black-crowned Night-Herons are found near marshes and along both freshwater and saltwater shores. During the day they roost in trees.

Voice The loud call of the Black-crowned Night-Heron is often heard when it flies at dusk or at night. It sounds like *quok!* or *quark!*

Food Black-crowned Night-Herons eat mostly fish, but they also hunt squid, crabs, crawfish, clams, mussels, frogs, snakes, and rodents. Some also eat the eggs or young of other birds.

SNOWY EGRET

The Snowy Egret is a beautiful white heron with fluffy white feathers and bright yellow feet. An active hunter, it may walk or run through shallow water or it may hover above the water and drop on its prey. Snowy Egrets sometimes use one of their feet to stir up the bottom to startle their prey. When the Snowy Egret sees movement, it strikes with its long bill.

Snowy Egrets were once hunted for their beautiful feathers, which were used to decorate hats. The number of Snowy Egrets dropped alarmingly and they were soon protected by law. Today their numbers have completely recovered. In fact, Snowy Egrets are now found in more places than they were before the hunting began.

Did You Know?
- The yellow feet of the Snowy Egret may attract fish.
- When Snowy Egrets build their nest, the male gathers materials and the female constructs the nest.
- All herons and egrets are protected by law.

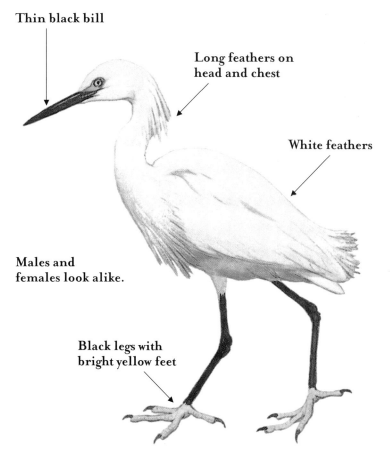

Thin black bill

Long feathers on head and chest

White feathers

Males and females look alike.

Black legs with bright yellow feet

Habitat Snowy Egrets are found hunting in both fresh water and salt water. They can be seen in swamps, marshes, ponds, and along shorelines.

Voice The sound most often made by a Snowy Egret is a kind of low croak. In its nesting colonies it makes noisy calls that sound like *wulla-wulla-wulla.*

Food Like other herons, Snowy Egrets catch a wide variety of fish, crabs, crayfish, frogs, lizards, and shrimp. They also eat insects, snails, and worms.

CATTLE EGRET

Cattle Egrets get their name from their habit of following large farm animals, such as cattle or horses, around fields. As the animals walk, they scare insects out of the grass, providing food for the egrets. Sometimes as many as eight Cattle Egrets will follow a single animal. They may even perch on a large animal's back.

Originally, Cattle Egrets were native only to Africa. Somehow they crossed the Atlantic Ocean and appeared in South America about 100 years ago. The first nesting pair in the United States was reported in 1952. Since then Cattle Egrets have spread across North America. They can now be seen in fields as far north as Canada.

Did You Know?
• In Africa Cattle Egrets hunt insects by following zebras, Cape buffaloes, and even elephants through the fields.
• Some Cattle Egrets migrate south from Canada as far as northern South America.

Yellow bill

Buff color
on head

Buff color
on back
and chest

Entirely
white

(Adult)

(Young)

Males and
females look alike.

Habitat Cattle Egrets are found in any kind of open country, along roadsides, in pastures, and on plowed fields and lawns. The can also be found in marshes and flooded fields.

Voice Cattle Egrets seldom make any sounds.

Food Although they usually hunt large insects such as grasshoppers and crickets, Cattle Egrets also eat frogs, spiders, and sometimes fish.

INDEX & LIFE LIST	*When*	*Where*
Brown Pelican, 14		
Canada Goose, 24		
Caspian Tern, 12		
Common Snipe, 36		
Coot, 16		
Double-crested Cormorant, 22		
Egrets		
Cattle Egret, 46		
Snowy Egret, 44		
Greater Yellowlegs, 38		
Gulls		
Herring Gull, 8		
Ring-billed Gull, 10		
Herons		
Black-crowned Night-Heron, 42		
Great Blue Heron, 40		
Killdeer, 34		
Mallard, 18		
Pintail, 20		
Sanderling, 28		
Sandpipers		
Least Sandpiper, 30		
Spotted Sandpiper, 32		
Swans		
Mute Swan, 26		
Tundra Swan, 26